THE GRANITE PAIL

THE
GRANITE
PAIL

THE SELECTED POEMS OF

Lorine Niedecker

Edited by Cid Corman

GNOMON

Frontispiece photograph by Gail Roub
taken in the fall of 1967, used with kind permission
of the photographer.

Library of Congress Catalogue Card Number:
96-75663

ISBN: 0-917788-61-3

Published by:
Gnomon Press
P. O. Box 475
Frankfort, Kentucky
40602-0475

PREFACE

Lorine Niedecker left me as her literary executor—without warning, since her death came upon her suddenly—as one of her ultimate conscious acts, and this could only have been because she knew I deeply shared her desire to let her work be known. She wrote clearly—despite the puzzled responses of her townsfolk—in a way that was near to "folk" literature. That is why she named her first collection of poems *New Goose:* not merely in self-deprecation but to relate her "rhymes" to America's first children's rhyme book, wanting them to be as "immediate," as fun, as memorable, as haunting as the best of that tradition.

All that she experienced in her life she brought into her poetry, which she understood as preciseness and conciseness brought to the pitch of music. She never quite cottoned to public reading of poetry (her only voicing was a tape I made of her at her home at the brink of Lake Koshkonong on her beloved Black Hawk Island—near where she had been born to working-class parents—under protest about six weeks before she died on the last day of 1970). For her, poetry was something each person had to read—say—get for himself or herself. Quiet music.

She was sixty-seven. She had hoped for more years for the poetry that remained within her. She was a gracious, self-effacing woman, small and seemingly self-contained, with thick glasses she had worn since childhood. She was candid both with others and with herself, although never tactless, for she was always aware of others and she felt an almost palpable happiness in the privilege of their presences. Her poetry appropriates voices more than history—the rock of true spirit and human relation.

At the same time, her poetry was permeated by a profound sense of *De Rerum Natura:* of nature's things. Among such things of nature—birds and rocks and weeds and flowers and the earth itself—she most loved trees, especially those she had watched her father plant along the island. Hers was a love that loved to know not only the name of this or that but also the nature of—the colors of—the seasons of—the relationships of everything to human life and the relationships of human life to all else. As she said to me at our one meeting about her husband, Al Millen (now also dead): "he dotes on science fiction but for me science seems more fictional than any story one could invent for it." She preferred it, as she preferred everything, clear-eyed and clear-spoken.

It is one of the features of her work: not only how she melds language and nature, the literal world within and without, but how she herself melds with those things and with the voices of those she was drawn to —so that one hears her always coming through (the wry). She has taken on the aspect of a larger, deeper voice—always nuanced by an incredible zest and joy—and equally stressed by an ever deepening sense of how the aches of livingdying wanted and warranted her passing through.

I have written many poems relating to her and think of her—in her own words and in our endless correspondence—constantly. My gratefulness to whatever gods there be that she shared some of her "life" with me—with us—perhaps you will grow also to feel. This recent poem (out of Bob Arnold's *Longhouse*) may cue you in:

> Suddenly
> a bird call
> makes it seem
>
> (I don't know
> why) like a
> holiday
>
> like getting
> a letter
> from Lorine.

Cid Corman, Kyoto, 1985

Now a decade later, one wants to note that interest in Lorine's work has grown immensely and that would have pleased her. Much of this is due to the continuing study of her work by Jenny Penberthy. Others who have contributed notably are—of course—Gail Roub, Glenna Breslin, Lisa Pater Faranda, Mike Heller, Kevin Oderman, Jerry Reisman, Carl Rakosi, Kristine Thatcher, Phyllis Walsh, Carole Beard, Nicolas Linkert, Douglas Crase, and a lengthening number. LN is now more and more represented in anthologies.

This edition has added six poems, cued in by readers, and the one typo ("name" for "mane") set right. Plus some minor revisions.

Cid Corman, Kyoto, November 6, 1995

CONTENTS

II. NORTH CENTRAL

III. HARPSICHORD & SALT FISH

.

EDITORIAL NOTE

The section headings are all vintage Niedecker, but they stake out the poems in three large masses. The earlier work—apprentice to Zukofsky but finding her voice; the central work—when she discovers her range and depth; the final work—much of it known posthumously—showing how she was probing other voices into a larger plenum.

There are variants on a number of poems. In every instance her own latest judgment has been given the nod.

All apparatus has been dispensed with for this edition. This is now available in *Lorine Niedecker: Collected Works* edited by Jenny Penberthy (University of California Press, 2002).

I

MY FRIEND TREE

There's a better shine
on the pendulum
than is on my hair
and many times

   • •   • •

I've seen it there.

My friend tree
I sawed you down
but I must attend
an older friend
the sun

Along the river
     wild sunflowers
over my head
     the dead
who gave me life
     give me this
our relative the air
     floods
our rich friend
     silt

Black Hawk held: In reason
land cannot be sold,
only things to be carried away,
and I am old.

Young Lincoln's general moved,
pawpaw in bloom,
and to this day, Black Hawk,
reason has small room.

Remember my little granite pail?
The handle of it was blue.
Think what's got away in my life—
Was enough to carry me thru.

The museum man!
I wish he'd take Pa's spitbox!
I'm going to take that spitbox out
and bury it in the ground
and put a stone on top.
Because without that stone on top
it would come back.

Mr. Van Ess bought 14 washcloths?
Fourteen washrags, Ed Van Ess?
Must be going to give em
to the church, I guess.

He drinks, you know. The day we moved
he came into the kitchen stewed,
mixed things up for my sister Grace—
put the spices in the wrong place.

Don't shoot the rail!
Let your grandfather rest!
Tho he sees your wild eyes
he's falling asleep,
his long-billed pipe
on his red-brown vest.

Asa Gray wrote Increase Lapham:
pay particular attention
to my pets, the grasses.

The clothesline post is set
yet no totem-carvings distinguish the Niedecker tribe
from the rest; every seventh day they wash:
worship sun; fear rain, their neighbors' eyes;
raise their hands from ground to sky,
and hang or fall by the whiteness of their all.

Well, spring overflows the land,
floods floor, pump, wash machine
of the woman moored to this low shore by deafness.

    Good-bye to lilacs by the door
    and all I planted for the eye.
    If I could hear—too much talk in the world,
    too much wind washing, washing
    good black dirt away.

Her hair is high.
Big blind ears.

    I've wasted my whole life in water.
    My man's got nothing but leaky boats.
    My daughter, writer, sits and floats.

Old man who seined
to educate his daughter
sees red Mars rise:
          What lies
behind it?

Cold water business
now starred in Fishes
of dipnet shape
          to ache
thru his arms.

You are my friend—
you bring me peaches
and the high bush cranberry
             you carry
my fishpole

you water my worms
you patch my boot
with your mending kit
          nothing in it
but my hand

Paul
　　when the leaves
　　　　fall

from their stems
　　that lie thick
　　　　on the walk

in the light
　　of the full note
　　　　the moon

playing
　　to leaves
　　　　when they leave

the little
　　thin things
　　　　Paul

Old Mother turns blue and from us,
   "Don't let my head drop to the earth.
I'm blind and deaf." Death from the heart,
   a thimble in her purse.

"It's a long day since last night.
   Give me space. I need
floors. Wash the floors, Lorine!—
   wash clothes! Weed!"

What horror to awake at night
and in the dimness see the light.
        Time is white
        mosquitoes bite
I've spent my life on nothing.

The thought that stings. How are you, Nothing,
sitting around with Something's wife.
        Buzz and burn
        is all I learn
I've spent my life on nothing.

I'm pillowed and padded, pale and puffing
lifting household stuffing—
        carpets, dishes
        benches, fishes
I've spent my life in nothing.

He lived—childhood summers
    thru bare feet
then years of money's lack
    and heat

beside the river—out of flood
    came his wood, dog,
woman, lost her, daughter—
    prologue

to planting trees. He buried carp
    beneath the rose
where grass-still
    the marsh rail goes.

To bankers on high land
    he opened his wine tank.
He wished his only daughter
    to work in the bank

but he'd given her a source
    to sustain her—
a weedy speech,
    a marshy retainer.

I knew a clean man
but he was not for me.
Now I sew green aprons
over covered seats. He

wades the muddy water fishing,
falls in, dries his last pay-check
in the sun, smooths it out
in *Leaves of Grass*. He's
the one for me.

In the great snowfall before the bomb
colored yule tree lights
windows, the only glow for contemplation
along this road

I worked the print shop
right down among em
the folk from whom all poetry flows
and dreadfully much else.

I was Blondie
I carried my bundles of hog feeder price lists
down by Larry the Lug,
I'd never get anywhere
because I'd never had suction,
pull, you know, favor, drag,
well-oiled protection.

I heard their rehashed radio barbs—
more barbarous among hirelings
as higher-ups grow more corrupt.
But what vitality!   The women hold jobs—
clean house, cook, raise children, bowl
and go to church.

What would they say if they knew
I sit for two months on six lines
of poetry?

Swept snow, Li Po,
by dawn's 40-watt moon
to the road that hies to office
away from home.

Tended my brown little stove
as one would a cow—she gives heat.
Spring—marsh frog-clatter peace
breaks out.

The graves

You were my mother, thorn apple bush,
armed against life's raw push.
But you my father catalpa tree
stood serene as now—he refused to see
that the other woman, the hummer he shaded
　　　　　hotly cared
for his purse petals falling—
　　　　　his mind in the air.

I rose from marsh mud,
algae, equisetum, willows,
sweet green, noisy
birds and frogs

to see her wed in the rich
rich silence of the church,
the little white slave-girl
in her diamond fronds.

In aisle and arch
the satin secret collects.
United for life to serve
silver.   Possessed.

My mother saw the green tree toad
on the window sill
her first one
since she was young.
We saw it breathe

and swell up round.
My youth is no sure sign
I'll find this kind of thing
tho it does sing.
Let's take it in

I said so grandmother can see
but she could not
it changed to brown
and town
changed us, too.

I am sick with the Time's buying sickness.
The overdear oil drum now flanged to my house
serves a stove costing as much.
I need a piano.

Then I'd sing "When to the sessions
of sweet silent thought"
true value expands
it warms.

I lost you to water, summer
when the young girls swim,
to the hot shore
to little peet-tweet-
        pert girls.

Now it's cold your bright knock
—Orion's with his dog after him—
at my door, boy
on a winter
        wave ride.

Hear
where her snow-grave is
the *You*
     ah you
of mourning doves

How white the gulls
in grey weather
      Soon April
      the little
yellows

New-sawed
clean-smelling house
sweet cedar pink
       flesh tint
I love you

Popcorn-can cover
screwed to the wall
over a hole
    so the cold
can't mouse in

Lights, lifts
parts nicely opposed
this white
            lice lithe
pink bird

O late fall
marsh—
              I
raped by the dry
weed stalk

Springtime's wide
water-
　　　yield
but the field
will return

July, waxwings
on the berries
have dyed red
      the dead
branch

People, people—
ten dead ducks' feathers
on beer can litter...
                    Winter
will change all that

Energy glows at the lips—
a cigarette—
measure the man pending...

under him droppings
larger, whiter than owls'—
What thought burns here?

1937

In the picture soldiers
moving thru a field
of flowers,
Spanish reds.
The flowers of war
move cautiously
not to tread
the wild heads.

Here we last,
lilacs, vacant lots,
taxes, no work,
debts, the wind widens
the grass.

In the old house
the clocks are dead,
past dead.

Depression Years

My daughters left home
I was job-certified
to rake leaves
                    in New Madrid.

Now they tell me my girls
should support me again
and they're not out of debt
                    from the last time they did.

Keen and lovely man moved as in a dance
to be considerate in lighted, glass-walled
almost outside office. Business

wasn't all he knew. He knew music, art.
Had a heart. "With eyes like yours I should think
the dictaphone" or did he say the flute?

His sensitivity—it stopped you.
And the neighbors said "She's taking lessons
on the dictaphone" as tho it were a saxophone.

He gave the job to somebody else.

Who was Mary Shelley?
What was her name
before she married?

She eloped with this Shelley
she rode a donkey
till the donkey had to be carried.

Mary was Frankenstein's creator
his yellow eye
before her husband was to drown

Created the monster nights
after Byron, Shelley
talked the candle down.

Who was Mary Shelley?
She read Greek, Italian
She bore a child

Who died
and yet another child
who died

I've been away from poetry
many months

and now I must rake leaves
with nothing blowing

between your house
and mine

II

NORTH CENTRAL

My life is hung up
in the flood
   a wave-blurred
     portrait

Don't fall in love
with this face—
   it no longer exists
     in water
       we cannot fish

Easter

A robin stood by my porch
and side-eyed
raised up
a worm

Get a load
        of April's
                fabulous

frog rattle—
        lowland freight cars
                in the night

Now in one year
   a book published
      and plumbing—
took a lifetime
  to weep
     a deep
        trickle

Dusk—

He's spearing from a boat—

How slippery is man
      in spring
            when the small fish
               spawn

Something in the water
like a flower
will devour

water

flower

The wild and wavy event
now chintz at the window

was revolution...
Adams

to Miss Abigail Smith:
You have faults

You hang your head down
like a bulrush

you read, you write, you think
but I drink Madeira

to you
and you cross your Leggs

while sitting.
(Later:)

How are the children?
If in danger run to the woods.

Evergreen o evergreen
how faithful are your branches

Linnaeus in Lapland

Nothing worth noting
except an Andromeda
with quadrangular shoots—
    the boots
of the people

wet inside: they must swim
to church thru the flood
or be taxed—the blossoms
    from the bosoms
of the leaves

Club 26

Our talk, our books
riled the shore like bullheads
at the roots of the luscious
large water lily

Then we entered the lily
built white on a red carpet

the circular quiet
cool bar

glass stems to caress

We stayed till the stamens trembled

In Leonardo's light
we questioned

the sun does not love
My hat

attained
the weight falls

I am at rest
You too

hold a doctorate
in Warmth

The men leave the car
to bring us green-white lilies
    by woods
These men are our woods
yet I grieve

I'm swamp
as against a large pine-spread—
his clear No marriage
    no marriage
friend

As praiseworthy

The power of breathing (Epictetus)
while we sleep. Add:
to move the parts of the body
without sound

and to float
on a smooth green stream
in a silent boat

Watching dan-
cers on skates

Ten thousand women
        and I
            the only one
                    in boots

Life's dance:
        they meet
            he holds her leg
                    up

As I paint the street

I melt the houses
to point up the turreted cupola
I make hoopla

of the low tavern's neon cross—
very like a cross from here—
I honor the huge blue distant dome
valid somehow to the fellow falling high

Some float off on chocolate bars
and some on drink

Harmless, happy, soft of heart

This bottle may breed
a new race
        no war
        and let birds live

Myself, I gripped my melting container
the night I heard the wild
wet rat, muskrat
grind his frogs and mice
the other side of a thin door
in the flood

Poet's work

Grandfather
  advised me:
    Learn a trade

I learned
  to sit at desk
    and condense

No layoff
  from this
    condensery

To my pres-
sure pump

I've been free
    with less
       and clean
I plumbed for principles

Now I'm jet-bound
by faucet   shower
heater   valve
ring seal   service

cost to my little
    humming
       water
          bird

Alcoholic dream
that ran him
          out from home
                    to return
leaning

like the house
in this old part
    of town leaves him
              grieving:
why

do I hurt you
whom I love?
    Your ear
       is cold!—here,
drink

Consider at the outset:
to be thin for thought
or thick cream blossomy

Many things are better
flavored with bacon

Sweet Life, My love:
didn't you ever try
this delicacy—the marrow
in the bone?

And don't be afraid
to pour wine over cabbage

LAKE SUPERIOR

In every part of every living thing
is stuff that once was rock

In blood the minerals
of the rock

Iron the common element of earth
in rocks and freighters

Sault Sainte Marie—big boats
coal-black and iron-ore-red
topped with what white castlework

The waters working together
        internationally
Gulls playing both sides

Radisson:
'a laborinth of pleasure'
this world of the Lake

Long hair, long gun

Fingernails pulled out
by Mohawks

(The long
canoes)

'Birch Bark
and white Seder
for the ribs'

Through all this granite land
the sign of the cross

Beauty: impurities in the rock

And at the blue ice superior spot
priest-robed Marquette grazed
azoic rock, hornblende granite
basalt the common dark
in all the Earth

And his bones of such is coral
raised up out of his grave
were sunned and birch bark-floated
to the straits

Joliet

Entered the Mississippi
Found there the paddlebill catfish
come down from The Age of Fishes

At Hudson Bay he conversed in latin
with an Englishman

To Labrador and back to vanish
His funeral gratis—he'd played
Quebec's Cathedral organ
so many winters

Ruby of corundum
lapis lazuli
from changing limestone
glow-apricot red-brown
carnelian sard

Greek named
Exodus-antique
kicked up in America's
Northwest
you have been in my mind
between my toes
agate

Wild Pigeon

Did not man
    maimed by no
        stone-fall

mash the cobalt
    and the carnelian
        of that bird

Schoolcraft left the Soo—canoes
US pennants, masts, sails
chanting canoemen, barge
soldiers—for Minnesota

Their South Shore journey
        as if Life's—
The Chocolate River
        The Laughing Fish
and The River of the Dead

Passed peaks of volcanic thrust
Hornblende in massed granite
Wave-cut Cambrian rock
painted by soluble mineral oxides
wave-washed and the rains
did their work and a green
running as from copper

Sea-roaring caverns—
Chippewas threw deermeat
to the savage maws
'*Voyageurs* crossed themselves
tossed a twist of tobacco in'

    Inland then
beside the great granite
gneiss and the schists

to the redolent pondy lakes'
lilies, flag and Indian reed
'through which we successfully
             passed'

The smooth black stone
I picked up in true source park
    the leaf beside it
once was stone

Why should we hurry
    home

I'm sorry to have missed
    Sand Lake
My dear one tells me
    we did not
We watched a gopher there

TRACES OF LIVING THINGS
"strange feeling of sequence" S.M.

Museum

Having met the protozoic
  Vorticellae
    here is man
Leafing towards you
  in this dark
    deciduous hall

Far reach
  of sand
    A man

bends to inspect
  a shell
    Himself

part coral
  and mud
    clam

TV

See it explained—
compound interest
and the compound eye
   of the insect

the wave-line
on shell, sand, wall
and forehead of the one
   who speaks

We are what the seas
have made us

longingly immense

the very veery
on the fence

What cause have you
to run my wreathed
rose words
off

you weed
you pea-blossom weed
in a folk
field

Stone
and that hard
contact—
the human

On the mossed
massed quartz
on which spruce
grew dense

I met him
We were thick
We said good-bye
on The Passing Years
River

The eye
of the leaf
into leaf
and all parts
         spine
into spine
neverending
         head
to see

For best work
you ought to put forth
        some effort
        to stand
in north woods
among birch

Smile
        to see the lake
           lay
        the still sky
And
        out for an easy
           make
        the dragonfly

Fall

We must pull
the curtains—
we haven't any
leaves

Years
   hearing and sight
      passing

walk
   to the Point—
      (between the waters)

—how live
   (with daughters?)
      at the end

Unsurpassed in beauty
this autumn day

The secretary of defence
knew precisely what

the undersecretary of state
was talking about

Human bean
and love-over-the-fence

just up
from swamp trouble

High class human
got no illumine

how a ten cent plant
winds aslant

around a post
Man, history's host

to trembles
in the tendrils

I'm a fool
can't take it cool

Ah your face
but it's whether
you can keep me warm

Sewing a dress

The need
these closed-in days

to move before you
smooth-draped
and color-elated

in a favorable wind

74

I walked
on New Year's Day

beside the trees
my father now gone planted

evenly following
the road

Each
            spoke

J. F. Kennedy after
    the Bay of Pigs

To stand up

black-marked tulip
not snapped by the storm

'I've been duped by the experts'

—and walk
the South Lawn

Mergansers
    fans
        on their heads

Thoughts on things
    fold unfold
        above the river beds

"Shelter"

Holed damp
cellar-black beyond
the main atrocities
my sense of property's
adrift

Not burned we sweat—
we sink to water Death
(your hand!—
this was land)
disowns

MY LIFE BY WATER

My life
   by water—
      Hear

spring's
   first frog
      or board

out on the cold
   ground
      giving

Muskrats
   gnawing
      doors

to wild green
   arts and letters
      Rabbits

raided
   my lettuce
      One boat

two—
   pointed toward
      my shore

thru birdstart
    wingdrip
        weed-drift

of the soft
    and serious—
        Water

PAEAN TO PLACE

And the place
was water

Fish
    fowl
        flood
    Water lily mud
My life

in the leaves and on water
My mother and I
           born
in swale and swamp and sworn
to water

My father
thru marsh fog
    sculled down
        from high ground
saw her face

at the organ
bore the weight of lake water
    and the cold—
he seined for carp to be sold
that their daughter

might go high
on land
      to learn
Saw his wife turn
deaf

and away
She
      who knew boats
          and ropes
no longer played

She helped him string out nets
for tarring
      And she could shoot
          He was cool
to the man

who stole his minnows
by night and next day offered
      to sell them back
          He brought in a sack
of dandelion greens

if no flood
No oranges—none at hand
      No marsh marigolds
          where the water rose
He kept us afloat

I mourn her not hearing canvasbacks
their blast-off rise
    from the water
        Not hearing sora
rail's sweet

spoon-tapped waterglass-
descending scale-
    tear-drop-tittle
        Did she giggle
as a girl?

His skiff skimmed
the coiled celery now gone
    from these streams
        due to carp
He knew duckweed

fall-migrates
toward Mud Lake bottom
    Knew what lay
        under leaf decay
and on pickerelweeds

before summer hum
To be counted on:
    new leaves
        new dead
leaves

He could not
—like water bugs—
    stride surface tension
    He netted
loneliness

As to his bright new car
my mother—her house
    next his—averred:
        A hummingbird
can't haul

Anchored here
in the rise and sink
    of life—
        middle years' nights
he sat

beside his shoes
rocking his chair
    Roped not 'looped
        in the loop
of her hair'

I grew in green
slide and slant
    of shore and shade
        Child-time—wade
thru weeds

Maples to swing from
Pewee-glissando
    sublime
        slime-
song

Grew riding the river
Books
    at home-pier
        Shelley could steer
as he read

I was the solitary plover
a pencil
    for a wing-bone
From the secret notes
I must tilt

upon the pressure
execute and adjust
    In us sea-air rhythm
'We live by the urgent wave
of the verse'

Seven-year molt
for the solitary bird
    and so young
Seven years the one
dress

for town once a week
One for home
    faded blue-striped
as she piped
her cry

Dancing grounds
my people had none
    woodcocks had—
    backland-
air around

Solemnities
such as what flower
    to take
    to grandfather's grave
unless

water lilies—
he who'd bowed his head
    to grass as he mowed
    Iris now grows
on fill

for the two
and for him
    where they lie
    How much less am I
in the dark than they?

Effort lay in us
before religions
    at pond bottom
        All things move toward
the light

except those
that freely work down
    to oceans' black depths
        In us an impulse tests
the unknown

River rising—flood
Now melt and leave home
    Return—broom wet
        naturally wet
Under

soak-heavy rug
water-bugs hatched—
    no snake in the house
        Where were they?—
she

who knew how to clean up
after floods
    he who bailed boats, houses
        Water endows us
with buckled floors

You with sea water running
in your veins sit down in water
    Expect the long-stemmed blue
        speedwell to renew
itself

O my floating life
Do not save love
    for things
        Throw *things*
to the flood

ruined
by the flood
    Leave the new unbought—
        all one in the end—
water

I possessed
the high word:
    The boy my friend
        played his violin
in the great hall

On this stream
my moonnight memory
    washed of hardships
        maneuvers barges
thru the mouth

of the river
They fished in beauty
    It was not always so
        In Fishes
red Mars

rising
rides the sloughs and sluices
    of my mind
        with the persons
on the edge

WINTERGREEN RIDGE

Where the arrows
    of the road signs
        lead us:

Life is natural
    in the evolution
        of matter

Nothing supra-rock
    about it
        simply

butterflies
    are quicker
        than rock

Man
    lives hard
        on this stone perch

by sea
    imagines
        durable works

in creation here
    as in the center
        of the world

let's say
        of art
                We climb

the limestone cliffs
        my skirt dragging
                an inch below

the knee
        the style before
                the last

the last the least
        to see
                Norway

or 'half of Sussex
        and almost all
                of Surrey'

Crete perhaps
        and further:
                'Every creature

better alive
        than dead,
                men and moose

and pine trees'
        We are gawks
                lusting

after wild orchids
    Wait! What's this?—
    sign:

Flowers
    loveliest
        where they grow

Love them enjoy them
    and leave them so
    Let's go!

Evolution's wild ones
    saved
        continuous life

through change
    from Time Began
    Northland's

unpainted barns
    fish and boats
        now this—

flowering ridge
    the second one back
        from the lighthouse

Who saved it?—
    Women
        of good wild stock

stood stolid
    before machines
        They stopped bulldozers

cold
    We want it for all time
        they said

and here it is—
    horsetails
        club mosses

stayed alive
    after dinosaurs
        died

Found:
    laurel in muskeg
        Linnaeus' twinflower

Andromeda
    Cisandra of the bog
        pearl-flowered

Lady's tresses
    insect-eating
        pitcher plant

Bedeviled little Drosera
    of the sundews
        deadly

in sphagnum moss
    sticks out its sticky
        (Darwin tested)

tentacled leaf
    toward a fly
        half an inch away

engulfs it
    Just the touch
        of a gnat on a filament

stimulates leaf-plasma
    secretes a sticky
        clear liquid

the better to eat you
    my dear
        digests cartilage

and tooth enamel
    (DHL spoke of blood
        in a green growing thing

in Italy was it?)
    They do it with glue
        these plants

Lady's slippers' glue
    and electric threads
        smack the sweets-seeker

on the head
    with pollinia
        The bee

befuddled
    the door behind him
        closed he must

go out at the rear
    the load on him
        for the next

flower
    Women saved
        a pretty thing: Truth:

'a good to the heart'
    It all comes down
        to the family

'We have a lovely
    finite parentage
        mineral

vegetable
    animal'
        Nearby dark wood—

I suddenly heard
    the cry
        my mother's

there the light
		pissed past
			the pistillate cone

how she loved
		closed gentians
			she herself

so closed
		and in this to us peace
			the stabbing

pen
		friend did it
			close to the heart

pierced the woods
		red
			(autumn?)

Sometimes it's a pleasure
		to grieve
			or dump

the leaves most brilliant
		as do trees
			when they've no need

of an overload
		of cellulose
			for a cool while

Nobody, nothing
    ever gave me
        greater thing

than time
    unless light
        and silence

which if intense
    makes sound
        Unaffected

by man
    thin to nothing lichens
        grind with their acid

granite to sand
    These may survive
        the grand blow-up—

the bomb
    When visited
        by the poet

from Newcastle on Tyne
    I neglected to ask
        what wild plants

have you there
    how dark
        how inconsiderate

of me
    Well I see at this point
        no pelting of police

with flowers
    no uprooted gaywings
        bishop's cup

white bunchberry
    under aspens
        pipsissewa

(wintergreen)
    grass of parnassus
        See beyond—

ferns
    algae
        water lilies

Scent
    the simple
        the perfect

order
    of that flower
        water lily

I see no space rocket
    launched here
        no mind-changing

acids eaten
　　one sort manufactured
　　　　as easily as gin

in a bathtub
　　Do feel however
　　　　in liver and head

as we drive
　　towards cities
　　　　the change

in church architecture—
　　now it's either a hood
　　　　for a roof

pulled down to the ground
　　and below
　　　　or a factory-long body

crawled out from a rise
　　of black dinosaur-necked
　　　　blower-beaked

smokestack-
　　steeple
　　　　Murder in the Cathedral's

proportions
　　Do we go to church
　　　　No use

discussing heaven
    HJ's father long ago
        pronounced human affairs

gone to hell
    Great God—
        what men desire!—

the scientist: a full set
    of fishes
        the desire to know

Another: to talk beat
    act cool
        release   la'go

So far out of flowers
    human parts found
        wrapped in newspaper

left at the church
    near College Avenue
        More news: the war

which 'cannot be stopped'
    ragweed pollen
        sneezeweed

whose other name
    Ambrosia
        goes for a community

Ahead—home town
    second shift steamfitter
        ran arms out

as tho to fly
    dived to concrete
        from loading dock

lost his head
    Pigeons
        (I miss the gulls)

mourn the loss
    of people
        no wild bird does

It rained
    mud squash
        willow leaves

in the eaves
    Old sunflower
        you bowed

to no one
    but Great Storm
        of Equinox

III

HARPSICHORD
& SALT FISH

TRADITION

I

The chemist creates
    the brazen
    approximation:
Life
    Thy will be done
    Sun

II

Time to garden
    before I
    die—
to meet
    my compost maker
    the caretaker
of the cemetery

Easter Greeting

I suppose there is nothing
so good as human
immediacy

I do not speak loosely
of handshake
                which is

                of the mind
or lilies—stand closer—
smell

Laundromat

Casual, sudsy
social love
at the tubs

After all, ecstasy
can't be constant

The radio talk this morning
was of obliterating
the world

I notice fruit flies rise
from the rind
of the recommended
melon

I married

in the world's black night
for warmth
   if not repose.
   At the close—
someone.

I hid with him
from the long range guns.
   We lay leg
   in the cupboard, head
in closet.

A slit of light
at no bird dawn—
   Untaught
   I thought
he drank

too much.
I say
   I married
   and lived unburied.
I thought—

Your erudition
the elegant flower
of which

my blue chicory
at scrub end
of campus ditch

illuminates

THOMAS JEFFERSON

I

My wife is ill!
And I sit
           waiting
for a quorum

II

Fast ride
his horse collapsed
Now *he* saddled walked

Borrowed a farmer's
unbroken colt
To Richmond

Richmond How stop—
Arnold's redcoats
there

III

Elk Hill destroyed—
Cornwallis
carried off 30 slaves

Jefferson:
Were it to give them freedom
he'd have done right

IV

Latin and Greek
my tools
to understand
humanity

I rode horse
away from a monarch
to an enchanting
philosophy

V

The South of France

Roman temple
'simple and sublime'

Maria Cosway
        harpist
on his mind

white column
and arch

VI

To daughter Patsy: Read—
read Livy

No person full of work
was ever hysterical

Know music, history
dancing

(I calculate 14 to 1
in marriage
she will draw
a blockhead)

Science also
Patsy

VII

Agreed with Adams:
send spermaceti oil to Portugal
for their church candles

(light enough to banish mysteries?:
three are one and one is three
and yet the one not three
and the three not one)

and send salt fish
U.S. salt fish preferred
above all other

VIII

Jefferson of Patrick Henry
backwoods fiddler statesman:

'He spoke as Homer wrote'
Henry eyed our minister at Paris—

the Bill of Rights hassle—
'he remembers...

in splendor and dissipation
he thinks yet of bills of rights'

IX

True, French frills and lace
for Jefferson, sword and belt

but follow the Court to Fontainebleau
he could not—

house rent would have left him
nothing to eat

> . . .

He bowed to everyone he met
and talked with arms folded

He could be trimmed
by a two-month migraine

and yet
      stand up

X

Dear Polly:
I said No—no frost

in Virginia—the strawberries
were safe

I'd have heard—I'm in that kind
of correspondence

with a young daughter—
if they were not

Now I must retract
I shrink from it

XI

Political honors
        'splendid torments'
'If one could establish
        an absolute power
of silence over oneself'

When I set out for Monticello
    (my grandchildren
        will they know me?)
How are my young
        chestnut trees—

XII

Hamilton and the bankers
would make my country Carthage

I am abandoning the rich—
their dinner parties—

I shall eat my simlins
with the class of science

or not at all
Next year the last of labors

among conflicting parties
Then my family

we shall sow our cabbages
together

XIII

Delicious flower
of the acacia

or rather

Mimosa Nilotica
from Mr. Lomax

XIV

Polly Jefferson, 8, had crossed
to father and sister in Paris

by way of London—Abigail
embraced her—Adams said

'in all my life I never saw
more charming child'

Death of Polly, 25,
Monticello

XV

My harpsichord
my alabaster vase
and bridle bit
bound for Alexandria
Virginia

The good sea weather
of retirement
The drift and suck
and die-down of life
but there is land

XVI

These were my passions:
Monticello and the villa-temples
I passed on to carpenters
bricklayers what I knew

and to an Italian sculptor
how to turn a volute
on a pillar

You may approach the campus rotunda
from lower to upper terrace
Cicero had levels

XVII

John Adams' eyes
            dimming
Tom Jefferson's rheumatism
                  cantering

XVIII

Ah soon must Monticello be lost
            to debts
      and Jefferson himself
                  to death

XIX

Mind leaving, let body leave
Let dome live, spherical dome
and colonnade

Martha (Patsy) stay
'The Committee of Safety
must be warned'

Stay youth—Anne and Ellen
all my books, the bantams
and the seeds of the senega root

NURSERY RHYME

As I nurse my pump

The greatest plumber
　　in all the town
from Montgomery Ward
rode a Cadillac carriage
　　by marriage
and visited my pump

A sensitive pump
　　said he
that has at times a proper
　　balance
　　of water, air
and poetry

THREE AMERICANS

John Adams is our man
but delicate beauty
touched the other one—

an architect
and a woman artist
walked beside Jefferson

Abigail
(long face horse-name)
cheesemaker

chicken raiser
wrote letters that John
and TJ could savour

THOMAS JEFFERSON INSIDE

Winter when no flower

The Congress away from home

Love is the great good use
one person makes of another
(Daughter Polly of the strawberry
letter)

Frogs sing—then of a sudden
all their lights go out

The country moves toward violets
and aconites

FORECLOSURE

Tell em to take my bare walls down
my cement abutments
their parties thereof
and clause of claws

Leave me the land
Scratch out: the land

May prose and property both die out
and leave me peace

HIS CARPETS FLOWERED

WILLIAM MORRIS

I

—how we're carpet-making
by the river
a long dream to unroll
and somehow time to pole
a boat

I designed a carpet today—
dogtooth violets
and spoke to a full hall
now that the gall
of our society's

corruption stains throughout
Dear Janey I am tossed
by many things
If the change would bring
better art

but if it would not?
O to be home to sail the flood
I'm possessed
and do possess
Employer

of labor, true—
to get done
the work of the hand...
I'd be a rich man
had I yielded

on a few points of principle
Item sabots
blouse—
I work in the dye-house
myself

Good sport dyeing
tapestry wool
I like the indigo vats
I'm drawing patterns so fast
Last night

in sleep I drew a sausage—
somehow I had to eat it first
Colorful shores—mouse ear...
horse-mint...The Strawberry Thief
our new chintz

II

Yeats saw the betterment of the workers
by religion—slow in any case
as the drying of the moon
He was not understood—
I rang the bell

for him to sit down
Yeats left the lecture circuit
yet he could say: no one
so well loved
as Morris

III

Entered new waters
Studied Icelandic:
At home last minute signs
to post:
Vetch

grows here—Please do not mow
We saw it—Iceland—the end
of the world rising out of the sea—
cliffs, caves like 13th century
illuminations

of hell-mouths
Rain squalls through moonlight
Cold wet
is so damned wet
Iceland's

black sand
Stone buntings'
fly-up-dispersion
Sea-pink and campion a Persian
carpet

DARWIN

I

His holy
    slowly
        mulled over
  matter

not all 'delirium
    of delight'
        as were the forests
  of Brazil

'Species are not
    (it is like confessing
        a murder)
  immutable'

He was often becalmed
    in this Port Desire by illness
        or rested from species
  at billiard table

As to Man
    'I believe Man...
        in the same predicament
  with other animals'

II

Cordilleras to climb—Andean
    peaks 'tossed about
        like the crust
of a broken pie'

Icy wind
    Higher, harder
        Chileans advised eat onions
for shortness of breath

Heavy on him:
    Andes miners carried up
        great loads—not allowed
to stop for breath

Fossil bones near Santa Fé
    Spider-bite-scauld
        Fever
Tended by an old woman

'Dear Susan…
    I am ravenous
        for the sound
of the pianoforte'

III

FitzRoy blinked—
        sea-shells on mountain-tops!
            The laws of change
    rode the seas

without the good captain
        who could not concede
            land could rise from the sea
    until—before his eyes

earthquake—
        Talcahuana Bay drained out—
            all-water wall
    up from the ocean

—six seconds—
        demolished the town
            The will of God?
    Let us pray

And now the Galapagos Islands—
        hideous black lava
            The shore so hot
    it burned their feet

through their boots
        Reptile life
            Melville here later
    said the chief sound was a hiss

A thousand turtle monsters
    drive together to the water
        Blood-bright crabs hunt ticks
on lizards' backs

Flightless cormorants
    Cold-sea creatures—
        penguins, seals
here in tropical waters

Hell for FitzRoy
    but for Darwin Paradise Puzzle
        with the jig-saw gists
beginning to fit

IV

Years…balancing
    probabilities
        I am ill, he said
    and books are slow work

Studied pigeons
    barnacles, earthworms
        Extracted seeds
    from bird dung

Brought home Drosera—
    saw insects trapped
        by its tentacles—the fact
    that a plant should secrete

an acid acutely akin
    to the digestive fluid
        of an animal! Years
    till he published

He wrote Lyell: Don't forget
    to send me the carcass
        of your half-bred African cat
    should it die

V

I remember, he said
    those tropical nights at sea—
        we sat and talked
  on the booms

Tierra del Fuego's
    shining glaciers translucent
        blue clear down
  (almost) to the indigo sea

(By the way Carlyle
    thought it was most ridiculous
        anyone should care
  whether a glacier

moves a little quicker
    or a little slower
        or moved at all)
  Darwin

sailed out
    of Good Success Bay
        to carcass-
  conclusions—

the universe
    not built by brute force
        but designed by laws
  The details left

to the working of chance
'Let each man hope
and believe
what he can'

A NOTE ON THE AUTHOR

LORINE NIEDECKER (1903-1970) spent most of her life on Black Hawk Island on Lake Koshkonong outside Fort Atkinson, Wisconsin. Her father, Henry, made a living seining carp from the Rock River. In 1922 Lorine attended Beloit College, but left after two years to return home in order to care for her mother, Theresa (Daisy), who had become deaf.

She worked from May 1928 until August 1930 at the local library in Fort Atkinson. From 1938 until 1942, Niedecker worked for the W.P.A., contributing to the book, *Wisconsin: A Guide to the Badger State* (Duell, Sloan & Pearce, 1941). In 1942 she wrote scripts for WHA, the local radio station in Madison. From 1944 until 1950 she worked as a stenographer and proofreader for a local printer, who published the journal, *Hoard's Dairyman*. Then from 1957 until 1963 she worked at a local hospital doing menial work. In 1963 she married Albert Millen and these last years would prove her most productive.

Despite magazine publication and praise from many writers and active correspondences with other poets such as Louis Zukofsky, William Carlos Williams, Cid Corman, and Jonathan Williams, she lived a largely isolated life—with the result that her poems were just becoming known at the end of her life.

Her books are *New Goose* (James A. Decker, 1946), *My Friend Tree* (Wild Hawthorn, 1961), *North Central* (Fulcrum, 1968), *T & G, The Collected Poems (1936-1966)* (Jargon, 1969), *My Life By Water, Collected Poems 1936-1968,* (Fulcrum,

1970), *Blue Chicory* (Elizabeth Press, 1976), *The Granite Pail* (North Point, 1985), *From This Condensery, The Complete Writing of Lorine Niedecker* (Jargon, 1985), *Harpsichord & Salt Fish* (Pig Press, 1991), *A Cookbook* (Longhouse, 1992), and the definitive *Lorine Niedecker: Collected Works* edited by Jenny Penberthy (University of California Press, 2002).

Two books of letters have also appeared: *"Between Your House and Mine," The Letters of Lorine Niedecker to Cid Corman, 1960 to 1970*, edited by Lisa Pater Faranda, (Duke, 1986) and *Niedecker and the Correspondence with Zukofsky 1931-1970*, edited by Jenny Penberthy (Cambridge, 1993).

A number of books and journals have appeared paying tribute to her work: *Epitaphs for Lorine*, edited by Jonathan Williams (Jargon, 1973); *Truck 16 —Lorine Niedecker Issue*, edited by David Wilk (1975); *The Full Note: Lorine Niedecker*, edited by Peter Dent (Interim Press, 1983); *Lorine Niedecker, An Original Biography* by Jane Shaw Knox (Dwight Foster Public Library); *Lorine Niedecker: The Solitary Plover* by Phyllis Walsh (Juniper Press, 1992); and *Lorine Niedecker: Woman and Poet*, edited by Jenny Penberthy (National Poetry Foundation, 1996).

This book has been set in
Adrian Frutiger's Meridien on a
Macintosh Quadra 650 in Quark 3.31
with help from The Typewright.
Printing by Thomson-Shore.